Over Ebey's

Elevated Views of
Ebey's Landing National Historical Reserve

M. Denis Hill

Copyright © 2016, M. Denis Hill

All photographs, text and design copyright M. Denis Hill

All right reserved, including the right to reproduce this book or portions thereof in any form or by any means, electronic or mechanical, including photocopying, recording, or by any information storage and retrieval system, without permission in writing from the publisher. Address all inquiries to M. Denis Hill, denis@whidbeypanoramas.com, www.whidbeypanoramas.com

Printed in U.S.A.

First edition

Cover photograph: Ebey's Prairie, Admiralty Inlet and the Olympics, by M. Denis Hill
Back cover photographs: Admiralty Head, Penn Cove, San de Fuca, Coupeville, Crockett Farm.

ISBN 978-0-9983719-0-0

A portion of the proceeds of each book sold is donated to The Friends of Ebey's Landing National Historical Reserve, a 501(c)(3) that works in cooperation with the Reserve's Trust Board and National Park Service to fund projects and programs that protect, preserve and enhance the cultural and natural resources and the visitor experience of Ebey's Landing National Historical Reserve. You can make tax-deductible contributions at www.friendsofebeys.org.

Follow the work of Denis Hill at https://www.facebook.com/WhidbeyPanoramasl/

Introduction

Ebey's Landing National Historical Reserve was established 20 years before I moved to Coupeville. Since my arrival in 1998, the landscapes, seascapes and structures of the Reserve have been the principal inspiration for my photography.

Over Ebey's is my effort to document those subjects from an unusual, elevated perspective. The experience of shooting from above reveals relationships between landmarks and spaces—relationships we simply cannot otherwise experience. It's how we discern the forest, not just the trees.

The Reserve encompasses 17,572 acres; this portfolio is representative—not exhaustive—in its depiction of the area. You will find it organized in a clockwise spiral, exploring first the periphery of the reserve, then Coupeville ("The Heart of Ebey's Reserve") and Penn Cove. Restrictions precluded flying cameras over National Park Service and Washington State Parks lands; I am therefore grateful to owners of adjacent properties who provided access that allowed me to include parks without violating restricted spaces.

Some of the included images are not strictly aerial, but are downward-looking views shot from elevated (but terrestrial) cameras. I decided to include them to round out the image collection. Others are composited into panoramas from multiple images, causing distortions. I hope that viewers will find it worth looking beyond those anomalies to gain the benefit of the expansive views offered via this mechanism.

Thanks to Ebey's Reserve Manager Kristen Griffin, Preservation Coordinator Sarah Steen and Outreach Coordinator Holly Richards, as well as Island County Historical Society Executive Director Rick Castellano and Archivist Sarah Aldrich; all of whom helped assure the accuracy of my descriptions. More than thanks to Karen Rothboeck, a.k.a., *The Coupeville Manual of Style* for her attention to detail. And, of course, thank you to everyone who has helped create and sustain the Reserve and the community—all who contribute to the gravity that draws us to this unique spot on Earth.

M. Denis Hill
November 5, 2016

Ebey's Prairie

The prairie named for Colonel Isaac Ebey endures in its role as the agricultural hub of the Reserve. It also frames majestic vistas of Admiralty Inlet and the Olympic Range. The prairie is an evolving tableau of farming activity that encourages frequent visits.

FAR LEFT: Ebey's Prairie is anchored by Smith family holdings. These including land once slated for development, sparking formation of the Reserve. ABOVE: Other major farming operations by the Sherman, Bishop and Engle families round out the prairie. LEFT: Another view of the Smith Farm.

NOTE: The images above and on the facing page show distortion, a result of compositing several exposures to show extremely wide views.

ABOVE: Here's a closer view of cattle barns representing an era when dairy farming was a major focus of area farms. An example of the evolving nature of the "rural working landscape" that defines the Reserve is the small lake on the right. Before drain tiles were installaed to maximize arable land in the prairie, it was a permanent body of water. The return of the lake (welcomed by waterfowl) resulted as 100-year-old drain tiles failed. TOP RIGHT: Contrasting colors of adjacent fields, looking north. FAR RIGHT: A view toward the iconic Ebey's Bluff. BOTTOM RIGHT: The paved section of the Kettles Trail parallels State Route 20 along cultivated fields.

ABOVE: Looking toward Admiralty Bay from the start of Engle Road, landmarks along the road include Prairie Bottom Farm, the Hancock farmstead and Jenne Farm. The Reuble Farm lies just over the ridge. FACING PAGE TOP LEFT: Ebey Road leads the eye from Sherman's Pioneer Farm to the prairie. FACING PAGE TOP RIGHT: Looking over Smith farmland, the Rebecca Road neighborhood is perched above the prairie. RIGHT: Sunnyside Cemetery and another Sherman farm. FACING PAGE CENTER: The barns of the Engle Farm anchor a corner of the prairie. FACING PAGE RIGHT: Above the Prairie Overlook.

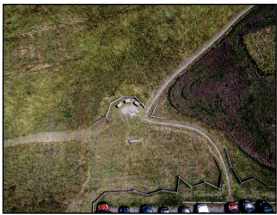

Ebey's Bluff to Point Partridge

This stretch of Whidbey Island's shoreline is unique, both in it's natural (seemingly undeveloped) appearance and its relative inaccessibility. State park land bounds this stretch at Ebey's Landing and Fort Ebey State Park. Developed uplands are largely hidden in the forest of native firs.

ABOVE: The Ebey's Bluff trail above Perego's Lagoon is a favorite hike. TOP LEFT: A Perego's Lagoon abstraction. TOP CENTER: Looking across Perego's Lagoon toward Victoria (hidden in fog). TOP RIGHT: Point Partridge. BOTTOM LEFT: Fort Ebey State Park from the Kettles direction. BOTTOM CENTER: Another view of Point Partridge BOTTOM RIGHT: At Lake Pondilla, Fort Ebey State Park offers beach access into a natural driftwood accumulation point.

Pebble Beach, Sierra, Lavender Wind Farm

Heading up the coast from Fort Ebey one encounters smaller neighborhoods south of Libbey Road, then the Sierra neighborhood and eventually Lavender Wind Farm.

FACING PAGE: Pebble Beach—between Ft. Ebey and Libbey Beach County Park—is a hidden gem on the west side. LEFT: The setting sun accentuates Lavender Wind Farm's colorful plants, with the Olympics in the distance. BELOW: Mt. Baker sits on the horizon in this view toward Sierra.

ABOVE: The Sierra neighborhood is known for views to the west. Here it is framed by a vew of Mt. Baker, the Cascades and Penn Cove (even a peek of Camano Island. RIGHT: Evening shadows highlight crops (some harvested and some just waiting) at Lavender Wind Farm.

Sky Meadows, San de Fuca

Above Grasser's Lagoon, the Sky Meadows neighborhood boasts enviable views along Penn Cove. San de Fuca is the historic anchor of the north shore of the cove.

FACING PAGE TOP: Grasser's Hill is now Sky Meadows, a neighborhood offering its own elevated views of Penn Cove and beyond. FACING PAGE BOTTOM: The San de Fuca schoolhouse from directly above. LEFT: The San de Fuca schoolhouse up close. BELOW: From San de Fuca to Blower's Bluff, and across Penn Cove to Long Point. Much of the San de Fuca area has been farmed by members of the Arnold family since 1907. The historic redbrick building above the cove—now home to Penn Cove Pottery—was originally a general store serving the area. Like Coveland, San de Fuca is an unincorporated place that was once expected to become a bona fide settlement.

Monroe's Landing, Blower's Bluff

Monroe's Landing is now enjoyed as a small county park with boat launch. Blower's Bluff guards the channel to Oak Harbor.

FACING PAGE: A natural point of access to Penn Cove, Monroe's Landing was the site of the last Native American longhouse on the cove. LEFT: A closer view of the neighborhoods above Monroe's Landing. BELOW: A landmark visible from across Penn Cove, Blower's Bluff is dominated by 3 Sisters Farm.

Snakelum Point, Long Point, Smith Prairie

Snakelum Point and Long Point were Native American settlements and traditional canoe landings for those headed to Smith Prairie.

ABOVE: Snakelum Point, named for old Chief Snetlun (aka Snakelum, d. 1850s) whose Lower Skagit Indian culture is well represented at the Island County Historical Society Museum in Coupeville. FACING PAGE TOP: Long Point was also an important Lower Skagit settlement. NEAR LEFT: Looking north toward Long Point and Blower's Bluff. FAR LEFT: Long Point and Snakelum Point ... and Mt. Baker across Saratoga Passage.

ABOVE: This view of Smith Prairie and beyond includes Pacific Rim Institute for Environmental Stewardship, the US Navy's outlying field, Admiralty Bay (top left), Penn Cove (top right) and the Olympic Range.

Keystone Spit, Crockett Lake, Crockett Farm

Keystone Spit looks out on Admiralty Bay. Crockett Lake is an important stop for migratory birds. The historic Crockett Farm looks across the lake.

FACING PAGE, LEFT: Hay awaiting bailing forms often-seen patterns. FACING PAGE RIGHT: The east end of Keystone Spit is developed with beachfront homes that lead to the Admirals Cove neighborhood. LEFT: The west end of Keystone Spit is largely occupied by Keystone State Park. Offshore is Keystone Underwater Park. BELOW LEFT: The historic house at the Crockett farmstead is now a bed and breakfast. BELOW: The post-and-beam construction Crockett Barn (in the style of a Pennsylvania bank barn) is both an historic landmark and a rural event center.

Fort Casey State Park, Camp Casey, Admiralty Head Light

Admiralty Head is flanked by Admiralty Inlet, Admiralty Bay and Crockett Lake. Fort Casey was sited here as part of the Triangle of Fire protecting Puget Sound.

FACING PAGE: Fort Casey State Park attracts visitors for views from Admiralty Head. The Admiralty Head Light is a popular subject for photographs. The gun emplacements guarding Admiralty Inlet are a tangible reminder of the strategic importance of Puget Sound. ABOVE: Camp Casey Conference Center was once part of the fort. Note how Keystone Spit divides Admiralty Bay from Crockett Lake.

ABOVE: Admiralty Head Light is one of Whidbey Island's popular sunset watching spots. FACING PAGE: Camp Casey Conference Center anchors a view that includes Admiralty Inlet Preserve, Crockett Lake and Crockett's Prairie.

Admiralty Inlet Preserve to Ferry House

Between Camp Casey and Ebey's Landing, Admiralty Inlet Preserve and the Cathedral Drive neighborhood crown the bluff.

FACING PAGE: Once part of Fort Casey, Whidbey Camano Land Trust's Admiralty Inlet Preserve includes the forest lower right in this photo. Cathedral Woods is the next body of trees, followed by Ebey's Landing. LEFT: A peek behind the Ferry House reveals the size of the rear wing. BELOW LEFT: The Ferry House backed by Cathedral Woods. BELOW: Late light on the Ferry House.

Coupeville, North of SR20
The larger, more developed segment of Coupeville is bounded by the Town Park bluff and Lovejoy Point.

FACING PAGE: The annual arts and crafts festival takes over downtown streets. The porch of the Island County Historical Society Museum (at right) looks over the festivities. LEFT: Penn Cove Mussel Farm and Admiralty Inlet are not far from the historic Coupeville Wharf. BELOW: Mt. Baker is often a jewel on the horizon, across Penn Cove.

ABOVE: Evening light adds a glow to the wharf, schooner Suva and all of the waterfront. FACING PAGE TOP LEFT: A behind the scenes perspective on the arts and crafts festival, looking over Front Street buildings. FACING PAGE TOP RIGHT: The view west along the cove starts at Captain Coupe Park and fades at Penn Cove Mussel Farm. FACING PAGE, BOTTOM: The view south follows (right to left) Alexander Street, Grace Street, Main Street, Center Street, Haller Street and Kinney Street. RIGHT: Some sunsets are more subtle than others.

ABOVE: In this exaggerated perspective, Lovejoy Point leads the eye to Long Point. FACING PAGE TOP: A view anchored by the transition from 9th Street to Parker Road includes Pennington Hill and out to Admiralty Bay. FACING PAGE BOTTOM: Homes in the Lovejoy Point area enjoy the best in-town sunset views.

LEFT: Whidbey Equestrian Center and the Strong farmstead mark the entrance to Coupeville from the south. BELOW: The barn at the base of this shot is on the Captain Coupe House property. The scene is rounded out with both historic and contemporary homes ... as well as town-owned land that has been envisioned as a major rain garden. FACING PAGE TOP: A panorama from atop Pennington Hill spans from WhidbeyHealth hospital on the left to the town's water storage tanks at right. FACING PAGE BOTTOM: This view from Pennington Hill places Ebey's Bluff top center.

Coupeville, South of SR20

Once known as Prairie Center, the south side of Coupeville is marked by schools, athletic fields and commercial development with a sprinkling of historic homes.

FACING PAGE: An 1890 farmhouse is bottom center in this shot, and Coupeville Storage would be hard to miss with its red roofing. ABOVE: At the south boundary of town looking north, several historic homes grace the west side of Main Street. LEFT: Still colloquially known as Prairie Center Grocery (or just "PC"), the town's market has been a hub of the south side since it was constructed in 1916. To the right is the local building supply emporium.

Mussel Farm to Captain Whidbey Inn

From the rafts of Penn Cove Mussel Farm, past Good Beach and Twin Lagoons, the majority of the Reserve lies between Penn Cove and Admiralty Inlet.

LEFT: Alpenglow illuminates Mt. Baker and Penn Cove.
BELOW: This view follows Madrona Way from Coupeville to the west end of Penn Cove, revealing, for example, a quarry and Good Beach, another spot favored by Native Americans.

FACING PAGE TOP: Looking east across Penn Cove Mussel Farm toward Saratoga Passage, Mt. Baker and the Cascades. FACING PAGE BOTTOM: Where the bodies known as Twin Lagoons connect with Penn Cove. LEFT: This perspective of the Captain Whidbey Inn reveals the proximity of the lagoons. BELOW: This view can be achieved by standing (well, flying) between those lagoons connections with the cove, turning your gaze from left to right.

For additional copies of *Over Ebey's* or to see more photography by M. Denis Hill, visit
www.whidbeypanoramas.com

This book is set in Century Gothic, a variant of Century suited to digital output.

PRINTED IN USA